MATERIALS TOWARD A BIBLIOGRAPHY OF THE WORKS OF TALBOT MUNDY

MATERIALS TOWARD A BIBLIOGRAPHY OF THE WORKS OF TALBOT MUNDY

EDITED BY

BRADFORD M. DAY

WILDSIDE PRESS

MATERIALS TOWARD A BIBLIOGRAPHY
OF THE WORKS OF TALBOT MUNDY

This edition published 2005 by Wildside Press, LLC
www.wildsidepress.com

CONTENTS

A BIT OF HIS LIFE 7

A LIST OF HIS BOOKS 11

A LIST OF HIS MAGAZINE STORIES 25

THE WALTER GALT STORIES 39

MUNDY'S SAGAS 41

READING SEQUENCE FOR SAGAS 45

THE JIMGRIM-RAMSDEN, et al, Saga 47

MONTE, ET AL, SAGA 53

TROS SAGA 55

A FINAL NOTE FROM THE EDITOR 57

A BIT OF HIS LIFE

Talbot Mundy was born in London on April 23, 1879. He was educated at Rugby, and served nearly ten years, beginning in 1900, as a government official in Africa and India. While in India, he wandered all over the sub-continent on horseback, and even into Tibet. Eastern occult lore first attracted, then fascinated, his active and unorthodox mind. Mundy absorbed all he could learn of the Indian beliefs.

Government service next brought him to Africa where he studied first-hand the nature magic of many of the tribes and cultures of East Africa. His quest for more information on this subject impelled him to travel extensively through Egypt and the Near East and even into parts of Arabia. This was truly adventurous at the time, but only in character with the man who killed dozens of lions and successfully hunted for ivory.

Mundy visited Australia, and Mexico as far south as Yucutan. He first arrived in the United States in 1911, and liked the country so much that he decided to stay and become a citizen.

Mundy quickly turned his energies to writing, and an article, "Pig Sticking in India," was accepted and published in the April 1911 issue of *Adventure* magazine, itself only a few months old. Another article and his first story, "The Phantom Battery" soon appeared. For years thereafter, *Adventure* had short stories, novelettes, novels, and serials by this master teller of tales in most of the issues that were printed.

The motif and locale of the stories and very infrequent articles usually stemmed from the areas, people, and occult knowledge previously mentioned. The manly art of self defense must have occupied some of Mundy's attention during his early career. A series of stories about Billy Blain, pugilist, appeared under the pen-name of Walter Gait, beginning with the February 1912 issue of *Adventure*. Two articles were also printed under this pseudonym.

Scribners of New York produced his first book, *Rung Ho*, in 1914, then apparently forgot him. In 1916, Bobbs-Merrill of Indianapolis published one of his most famous stories, *King — of the Khyber Rifles*, and Cassell and Company of London brought out *The Winds of the World*. Both were well received, and Mundy's career to a moderate renown was on its way.

In succeeding years he continued to write for *Adventure* and other magazines, most of the stories being snapped up by various book publishers. Many of the books were reprinted in several editions by different companies, and, confusing to a bibliophile, the English publications ware often re-titled.

During the 1920's Mundy bought a part of the Point Loma estate in California, called The Cliffs. He settled there for several years and became a member of the Theosophical Society presided over by Katherine Tingley. A half-dozen of his books were written there and, *Om; the Secret of Ahbor Valley*, shows the influence of this occult society.

He contributed many articles to Tingley's theosophical magazines, her most noted publication being the Theosophical Path. After her death in 1929, Mundy left Point Loma but always retained his interest in and sympathy with Theosophy.

Mundy continued writing almost to the time of his death on August 5, 1940. In all, forty-nine books were produced under his name, thirty-nine of which were original works. At least one-hundred and fifty stories and articles appeared in magazines; most of these, perhaps nearly all, are listed in this bibliography. None of the theosophical articles are included here, though, as the intent of this listing is to stress his mastery of the fantasy-high adventure tale.

It is still too soon to properly evaluate Mundy's importance in the stream of literature. His style of writing, choice of language, is smoothly readable. One "fault," if such it be, is a sometimes too carefully contrived buildup to plot situations. This careful skill did result in glowing word-pictures and living characters.

Considerable assistance was given on this project by friends and fellow enthusiasts. My grateful thanks to all as they come to mind:

Dr. J. Lloyd Eaton — Berkeley, California
John C. Nitka — Richmond Hill, New York
James A. Strand — Portland, Oregon
Walter A. Carrithers, Jr. — Fresno, California
Robert Resch — Reading, Pennsylvania
Richard Witter, Donald Grant, and some others for
              appreciated words of caution and advice.

The following list must not be supposed the final and authoritative word on this subject.

A LIST OF HIS BOOKS

ALL FOUR WINDS: FOUR NOVELS OF INDIA
  · Hutchinson London 1934 1232
    Cover Black — yellow letters

> *King – of the Khyber Rifles*
> *Jimgrim*
> *Om; the Secret of Ahbor Valley*
> *Black Light*

BLACK LIGHT
  · Bobbs-Merrill Indianapolis 1930 315
  · A.L. Burt

  Cover maroon – black letters

  ("There was no moon yet ...")

THE BUBBLE REPUTATION
  (See ibid — HER REPUTATION)

CAESAR DIES
  · Hutchinson London No date 206

  Cover red

  ("Golden Antioch lay like a jewel at a mountain's
    throat...")
  (The Falling Star – MAGAZINE – *Adventure* 10/23/26)

THE CAVES OF TERROR
  · Hutchinson London No date 255
  · (Pocketbook) Doubleday, Page New York 1924 118

  Cover light blue – rose letters

  ("Meldrum Strange has a way with him ...")

(The Gray Mahatma — MAGAZINE — *Adventure*
11/10/22 *Famous Fantastic Mysteries* 12/51)

C.I.D.

- Century New York 1932 280
- Hutchinson London 1932 288

Cover yellow — black letters with red and black
Oriental Figure

("It was typical south-west monsoon weather ...")
(C.I.D. — MAGAZINE — *Adventure* 3/1/33 to 4/15/33)

COCK O' THE NORTH

- Bobbs-Merrill Indianapolis 1929 340

Cover orange — black letters

("Angus, nicknamed 'Gup' McLeod, six feet two and a
half inches of him, came untouched out of the
Great War...")
(The Invisible Guns of Kabul — MAGAZINE —
Adventure 10/1/29)

THE DEVIL'S GUARD

- Bobbs-Merrill Indianapolis 1926 335
- Oriental Club
- Wells & Shakespeare

Cover maroon — green letters

("I find myself wondering why I should go to the
trouble to write what few men will believe ...")
(Ramsden — MAGAZINE — *Adventure* 6/8/26)

DIAMONDS SEE IN THE DARK

- Hutchinson London No date 287

Cover red

(See ibid — EAST AND WEST)

EAST AND WEST
- Appleton-Century New York 1937 310

  Cover yellow — black letters with red and black
  Oriental Figure

  ("Moses Lafayette O'Leary tossed his pith helmet to a
  coolie ...")

THE EYE OF ZEITOON
- Bobbs-Merrill Indianapolis 1920 354
- McKinley, Stone & McKenzie[A]
- A.L. Burt

  Cover reddish-brown — brown letters on black
  background

  ("It is written with authority of Tarsus that once it was
  no mean city ...")
  (The Eye of Zeitoon — MAGAZINE — Romance 2/20)

  [Footnote A: Masterpieces of Oriental Mystery — A set
  of ten titles]

FULL MOON
- Appleton-Century New York 1935 312

  Cover yellow — black letters with red and black
  Oriental Figure

  ("Bombay sweltered ...")
  (Full Moon — MAGAZINE — Famous Fantastic
  Mysteries 2/53)

THE GUNGA SAHIB
- Century New York and London 1934 303

  Cover yellow-black letters

  ("Birds sang blithely at the forest's edge ...")

(When Trails Were New — MAGAZINE —
Argosy-All-Story 10/27/28 to 12/1/28)

GUNS OF THE GODS
- Bobbs-Merrill Indianapolis 1921 359
- McKinley, Stone & McKenzie (Masterpieces of Oriental Mystery)

Cover yellow brown — black letters

("The why and wherefore of my privilege to write a true
account of the Princess Yasmini's Early youth is a
story ...")
(Guns of the Gods — MAGAZINE — *Adventure* 3/1/21
to 5/1/21)

GUP-BAHADUR
- Hutchinson London No date 292

Cover blue

(See ibid — COCK O' THE NORTH)

HER REPUTATION
- Bobbs-Merrill Indianapolis 1923 333
- A.L. Burt

Cover red — gold letters (Burt edition)

("There is an hour of promise and a zero hour ...")

HIRA SINGH'S TALE — When India came to fight in Flanders
- Bobbs-Merrill Indianapolis 1918 308
- McKinley, Stone & McKenzie (Masterpieces of Oriental Mystery)
- A.L. Burt

Cover green with embossed letters

("A Sikh who must have stood six feet without his
turban ...")

(Hira Singh's Tale — MAGAZINE — *Adventure*
10/18/17 to 12/3/17)

THE HUNDRED DAYS & THE WOMAN AYISHA
- Century New York and London 1931 349

Cover yellow — black letters with red and black
Oriental Figure

("They kept this out of the papers at the time ...")
(The Hundred Days — MAGAZINE — *Adventure*
4/10/22)
(The Woman Ayisha — MAGAZINE — *Adventure*
4/20/22)

I SAY SUNRISE
- Dakers London 1947 182
- Wells Philadelphia 1949 187

Wells edition cover dark blue — gold figure — gold
letters on spine

("I know whereof I write and to whom I write ...")
(Philosophical non-fiction)

THE IVORY TRAIL

- Bobbs-Merrill Indianapolis 1919 411 Ill.
- McKinley, Stone & McKenzie (Masterpieces of Ori-
ental Mystery)
- A.L. Burt

Cover red — red letters on black background

("Estimates of ease and affluence vary with the point of
view.")
(On the Trail of Tipoo Tib — MAGAZINE — *Adventure*
5/1/19
(Trek East — POCKETBOOK — Universal Pub. 1954)
to 7/15/19)

JIMGRIM

- Century New York and London 1931 385
- A.L. Burt

Cover yellow — black letters with red and black
Oriental Figure

("It was one of those sun-drunken days in spring ...")
(King of the World — MAGAZINE — *Adventure*
11/15/30 to 2/15/31)
(Jimgrim Sahib — POCKETBOOK — Universal Pub.
1953)

JIMGRIM AND ALLAH'S PEACE

- Appleton-Century New York 1936 279

Cover yellow — black letters with red end black
Oriental Figure

("There is a beautiful belief that journalists may do as
they
(The Adventure at El-Kerak — MAGAZINE — please...")
Adventure 11/10/21)
(Under the Dome of the Rock — Magazine — *Adventure*
12/10/21)

JUNGLE JEST

- Century New York and London 1932 392

Cover yellow — black letters

("Someone began to pray in a nasal snarl, and a
stallion
(Benefit of Doubt — MAGAZINE — *Adventure* squealed
...") 12/10/22)

THE KING IN CHECK

- Appleton-Century New York 1934 244
- Hutchinson London 1933 256

Appleton-Century edition cover purple — gold letters

("Whoever invented chess understood the world's
 works ...")
(The King in Check — MAGAZINE — *Adventure*
 7/10/22)

KING — OF THE KHYBER RIFLES

- Bobbs-Merrill Indianapolis 1916 395
- McKinley, Stone & McKenzie (Masterpieces of Ori-
  ental Mystery)
- Readers League of America
- A.L. Burt

> Cover red — red letters on black background
> Cover olive — gold letters
>   Variants of same edition?

> ("The men who govern India — more power to them
> and her ...")
> (King — of the Khyber Rifles — MAGAZINE —
> Everybody's 5/16)

THE LION OF PETRA

- Hutchinson London 1932 255
- Appleton-Century
- A.L. Burt

> ("This isn't an animal story ...")
> (The Lion of Petra — MAGAZINE — *Adventure*
> 3/10/22)

THE LOST TROOPER

- Hutchinson London No date 252

> Cover red — gold letters

> ("How can you begin a tale at the beginning when it
> has ...")
> (The Lost Trooper — MAGAZINE — *Adventure* 5/30/22)

THE MARRIAGE OF MELDRUM STRANGE

- Hutchinson London No date 254

Cover blue

("This is an immoral story ...")
(The Marriage of Meldrum Strange — MAGAZINE —
Adventure 10/10/23)

THE MYSTERY OF KHUFU'S TOMB
- Appleton-Century New York 1935 279 Ill.

Cover purple — gold letters

("We Americans are ostriches ...")
(Khufu's Real Tomb — MAGAZINE — *Adventure*
10/10/22)

THE NINE UNKNOWN
- Bobbs-Merrill Indianapolis 1923 353
- McKinley, Stone & McKenzie (Masterpieces of Oriental Mystery)

Cover blue — yellow letters

("I had this story from a dozen people ...")
(The Nine Unknown — MAGAZINE — *Adventure*
3/20/23 to 4/30/23)

OLD UGLY FACE
- Appleton-Century New York 1940 544
- Wells & Shakespeare

Cover blue — gold letters

("Things seemed vague that evening ...")

OM; THE SECRET OF AHBOR VALLEY
- Bobbs-Merrill Indianapolis 1924 392
- McKinley, Stone & McKenzie (Masterpieces of Oriental Mystery)
- Hutchinson

Cover green — black letters

("If you want views about the world's news, read what
...")
(Om; the Secret of Ahbor Valley — MAGAZINE —
Adventure 10/10/24 to 10/30/24)

PURPLE PIRATE
· Appleton-Century New York 1935 367

Cover yellow — black letters with red and black
Oriental Figure

("Hitherto I have found my real goal unattainable ...")
(Battle Stations — MAGAZINE — *Adventure* 5/1/35
Cleopatra's Promise *Adventure* 6/15/35
Purple Pirate *Adventure* 8/15/35
Fleets of Fire *Adventure* 10/1/35)

QUEEN CLEOPATRA
· Bobbs-Merrill Indianapolis 1929 426

Cover black — green letters

("Cleopatra yawned ...")

RAMSDEN
(See ibid — THE DEVIL'S GUARD)

THE RED FLAME OF ERINPURA
· Hutchinson London No date 255

Cover red

("There was a voice outside, and nothing else ...")
(The Red Flame of Erinpura — MAGAZINE —
Adventure 1/1/27)

ROMANCES OF INDIA
· A.L. Burt New York and Chicago No date 281

Cover orange — black letters

King – of the Khyber Rifles
Guns of the Gods
Told in the East

RUNG HO

- Scribners New York 1914 371 Ill.
- McKinley, Stone & McKenzie (Masterpieces of Oriental Mystery)
- A.L. Burt

Cover olive – black letters on front, gold on spine

("That was no time or place for any girl of twenty to ...")
(For the Peace of India – MAGAZINE – *Adventure* 2/14 to 4/14)

THE SEVENTEEN THIEVES OF EL KALIL

- Hutchinson London No date 254

Cover red

("Steam never killed romance ...")
(The Seventeen Thieves of El Kalil – MAGAZINE – *Adventure* 2/20/22)

THE SOUL OF A REGIMENT

- Alex Dulfer San Francisco 1925 25

Cover green – white spine

(See ibid – THE VALIANT VIEW)
(See ibid – ADVENTURE'S BEST STORIES – 1926 edited by A.S. Hoffman, an anthology published by Doran, New York, 1926)

(The Soul of A Regiment – MAGAZINE – *Adventure* 2/12)
("So long as its colours remain ...")

THERE WAS A DOOR

(See ibid – FULL MOON)

THE THUNDER DRAGON GATE
- Appleton-Century New York and London 1937 335
- Hutchinson

    Cover yellow — black letters with red and black
    Oriental Figure

    ("It was one of those days when not even Cockneys like
    London.")

TOLD IN THE EAST
- Bobbs-Merrill Indianapolis 1920 281
- McKinley, Stone & McKenzie (Masterpieces of Oriental Mystery)

    Cover brown — tan letters with black background

    ("A blood red sun rested its huge disc upon a low mud
    wall ...")
    (Hookum Hai — MAGAZINE — *Adventure* 7/13
    For the Salt He Had Eaten *Adventure* 3/13
    Machassan Ah *Adventure* 4/15)

TROS OF SAMOTHRACE
- Appleton-Century New York and London 1934 949

    Cover yellow — black letters

    (Tros of Samothrace — MAGAZINE — *Adventure*
    2/10/25
    The Enemy of Rome *Adventure* 4/10/25
    Prisoners of War *Adventure* 6/10/25
    Admiral of Caesar's Fleet *Adventure* 10/10/25
    The Dancing Girls of Gades *Adventure* 12/10/25
    A Messenger of Destiny *Adventure* 2/10/26 to 2/30/26)

THE VALIANT VIEW: a collection of stories
- Hutchinson London 1939 256

    Cover red

("So long as its colours remain, and there is one man
      left ...")
(The Soul of A Regiment — MAGAZINE — *Adventure*
      2/12
The Damned Old Nigger *Adventure* 5/16;
The Chaplain of the Hullingars *Adventure* 3/12
The Pillar of Light
One Arabian Fight *Adventure* 11/13
Machassan Ah *Adventure* 4/15
The Man from Poonch *Argosy* 6/17/33
The Eye-Teeth of O'Hara *Adventure* 11/1/31
Innocent Non-combatant
The Honorable Pig)

W.H.

- Hutchinson London No date 256

  Cover orange

  ("The manuscript of this story was found in the cellar
        of ...")
  (Ho for London Town — MAGAZINE — *Argosy-All-Story*
        2/2/29)
  (The Queen's Warrant — POCKETBOOK) 2/23/29)

WHEN TRAILS WERE NEW
- Hutchinson London No date 288

  (See ibid — THE GUNGA SAHIB)

THE WINDS OF THE WORLD
- Cassell London and New York 1916 307
- Bobbs-Merrill Indianapolis 1917 331 Ill.
- McKinley, Stone & McKenzie (Masterpieces of Oriental Mystery)
- A.L. Burt

  Cover light gray with turbaned figure

  ("A watery July sun was hurrying towards a Punjab
        skyline ...")
  (The Winds of the World — MAGAZINE — *Adventure*
        7/15 to 9/15)

THE WOMAN AYISHA

- Hutchinson London No date 256

    Cover red

    (See ibid — THE HUNDRED DAYS & THE WOMAN
        AYISHA)
    ("Consider the situation for a moment first ...")
    (The Woman Ayisha — MAGAZINE — *Adventure*
        4/20/22)

THE MAN FROM JUPITER

    (Is this an imaginary book?)

Claims have been advanced that Mundy wrote this work of science fiction. Doubtlessly most of the imaginative creation connected with this book is in the minds of the gulls who pass the name of this title along.

A LIST OF HIS MAGAZINE STORIES

PIGSTICKING IN INDIA
  Adventure — 1911 — April Article

SINGLE-HANDED YACHTING
  Adventure — 1911 — JulyArticle

THE PHANTOM BATTERY
  Adventure — 1911 — August

THE BLOODING OF THE NINTH QUEEN'S OWN
  Adventure — 1911 — December

FOR VALOUR
  Adventure — 1912 — January

THE SOUL OF A REGIMENT
  Adventure — 1912 — February
  Reprinted: April 1917 — November 1935 — November 1940
  (The Soul of A Regiment — BOOK)
  (The Valiant View — BOOK)
  (*Adventure's Best Stories* — 1926 — BOOK)

THE CHAPLAIN OF THE MULLINGARS
  Adventure — 1912 — March
  (The Valiant View — BOOK)

W. MAYES — THE AMAZING
  Adventure — 1912 — April Article

THE QUEEN — GOD BLESS HER
Adventure — 1912 — May

T.C. ANSELL — ADVENTURER
Adventure — 1912 — June

THE COWARDS
Adventure — 1912 — July

THE PAYMENT OF QUINN'S DEBT
Adventure — 1912 — August

IN WINTER QUARTERS
Adventure — 1912 — September

THE MAN WHO SAW
Adventure — 1912 — October

HONOR
Adventure — 1912 — November

RABBIT
Adventure — 1912 — December

THREE HELIOS
Adventure — 1913 — January

A LOW-VELDT FUNERAL
Adventure — 1913 — February Article

FOR THE SALT WHICH HE HAD EATEN
Adventure — 1913 — March
(Told in the East — BOOK)

PRIVATE MURDOCH'S G.C.M.
Adventure — 1913 — April

THE GUZZLER'S GRAND PRIX
Adventure — 1913 — May

AT MANEUVERS
Adventure — 1913 — June

HOOKUM HAI
Adventure — 1913 — July
(Told in the East — BOOK)

THE CLOSED TRIAL OF WM. WALKER
Adventure — 1913 — August Article

THE LETTER OF HIS ORDERS
Adventure — 1913 — September

IN A RIGHTEOUS CAUSE
Adventure — 1913 — October

AN ARABIAN NIGHT
Adventure — 1913 — November
(The Valiant View — BOOK)

THE TEMPERING OF HARRY BLUNT
Adventure — 1913 — December

A SOLDIER AND A GENTLEMAN
Adventure — 1914 — January

FOR THE PEACE OF INDIA
Adventure — 1914 — February to April (Serial, 3 parts)
(Rung Ho — BOOK)

THE GENTILITY OF IKEY BLUMENDALL
Adventure — 1914 — June

GULBAZ AND THE GAME
Adventure — 1914 — July

THE SWORD OF ISKANDER
Adventure — 1914 — August

FOUL OF THE CZAR
Adventure — 1914 — September

"GO, TELL THE CZAR!"
Adventure — 1914 — October

KING DICK
Adventure — 1914 — November

LANCING THE WHALE
Adventure — 1914 — December

DISOWNED!
Adventure — 1915 — January

NO NAME
Adventure — 1915 — February

ON TERMS
Adventure — 1915 — March

MACHASSAN AH
Adventure — 1915 — April
(The Valiant View — BOOK)
(Told in the East — BOOK)

A TEMPORARY TRADE IN TITLES
Adventure — 1915 — May

THE DOVE WITH A BROKEN WING
Adventure — 1915 — June

THE WINDS OF THE WORLD
Adventure — 1915 — July to September (Serial 3 parts)
(The Winds of the World — BOOK)

A DROP OR TWO OF WHITE TUCKER'S TONGUE
Adventure — 1916 — February Anecdote

THE DAMNED OLD NIGGER
Adventure — 1916 — May
(The Valiant View — BOOK)

KING — OF THE KHYBER RIFLES
Everybody's — 1916 — May
(King — of the Khyber Rifles — BOOK)

HIRA SINGH'S TALE
Adventure — 1917 — October 18 to December 3 (Serial 4 parts)
(Hira Singh's Tale — BOOK)

BLIGHTY
Adventure — 1918 — August 18 Article

OAKES RESPECTS AN ADVERSARY
Adventure — 1918 — December 3

AMERICA HORNS IN
Adventure — 1919 — January 3

JACKSON TACTICS
Adventure — 1919 — February 18

HEINIE HORNS INTO THE GAME
Adventure — 1919 — March 18

THE END OF THE BAD SHIP BUNDESRATH
Adventure — 1919 — April 18

ON THE TRAIL OF TIPOO TIB
Adventure — 1919 — May 3 to July 18 (Serial 6 parts)
(The Ivory Trail — BOOK)

THE SHRIEK OF DUM
Adventure — 1919 — September 3

BARABBAS ISLAND
Adventure — 1919 — October 18

IN ALEPPO BAZAAR
Adventure — 1919 — December 18

THE EYE OF ZEITOON
Romance — 1920 — February
(The Eye of Zeitoon — BOOK)

GUNS OF THE GODS
Adventure — 1921 — March 3 to May 3 (Serial 5 parts)
(Guns of the Gods — BOOK)

THE ADVENTURE AT EL-KERAK
Adventure — 1921 — November 10
(Jimgrim and Allah's Peace — BOOK)

UNDER THE DOME OF THE ROCK
Adventure — 1921 — December 10
(Jimgrim and Allah's Peace — BOOK)

THE "IBLIS" AT LUDD
Adventure — 1922 — January 10

THE SEVENTEEN THIEVES OF EL-KALIL
Adventure — 1922 — February 20

(The Seventeen Thieves of El-Kalil — BOOK)

THE LION OF PETRA
Adventure — 1922 — March 10
(The Lion of Petra — BOOK)

THE HUNDRED DAYS
Adventure — 1922 — April 10
(The Hundred Days & The Woman Ayisha — BOOK)

THE WOMAN AYISHA
Adventure — 1922 — April 20
(The Hundred Days & The Woman Ayisha — BOOK)
(The Woman Ayisha — BOOK)

THE LOST TROOPER
Adventure — 1922 — May 30
(The Lost Trooper — BOOK)

THE KING IN CHECK
Adventure — 1922 — July 10
(The King in Check — BOOK)

A SECRET SOCIETY
Adventure — 1922 — August 10

MOSES & MRS. AINTREE
Adventure — 1922 — September 10

KHUFU'S REAL TOMB
Adventure — 1922 — October 10
(The Mystery of Khufu's Tomb — BOOK)

THE GRAY MAHATMA
Adventure — 1922 — November 10
Reprinted: Famous Fantastic Mysteries — 1951 — December

(The Caves of Terror — BOOK)

BENEFIT OF DOUBT
Adventure — 1922 — December 10
(Jungle Jest — BOOK)

TREASON
Adventure — 1923 — January 10

THE NINE UNKNOWN
Adventure — 1923 — March 20 to April 30 (Serial 5 parts)
(The Nine Unknown — BOOK)

DIANA AGAINST THE EPHESIANS
Adventure — 1923 — August 10

THE MARRIAGE OF MELDRUM STRANGE
Adventure — 1923 — October 10
(The Marriage of Meldrum Strange — BOOK)

MOHANNED'S TOOTH
Adventure — 1923 — December 10

OM; THE SECRET OF AHBOR VALLEY
Adventure — 1924 — October 10 to November 30 (Serial 6 parts)
(Om; the Secret of Ahbor Valley — BOOK)

TROS OF SAMOTHRACE
Adventure — 1925 — February 10
(Tros of Samothrace — BOOK)

THE ENEMY OF ROME
Adventure — 1925 — April 10
(Tros of Samothrace — BOOK)

PRISONERS OF WAR
>   *Adventure* — 1925 — June 10
>   (Tros of Samothrace — BOOK)

ADMIRAL OF CAESAR'S FLEET
>   *Adventure* — 1925 — October 10
>   (Tros of Samothrace — BOOK)

THE DANCING GIRLS OF GADES
>   *Adventure* — 1925 — December 10
>   (Tros of Samothrace — BOOK)

THE MESSENGER OF DESTINY
>   *Adventure* — 1926 — February 10, 20, 30 (Serial 3 parts)
>   (Tros of Samothrace — BOOK)

RAMSDEN
>   *Adventure* — 1926 — June 8 to August 8 (Serial 5 parts)
>   (The Devil's Guard — BOOK)
>   (Ramsden — BOOK)

THE FALLING STAR
>   *Adventure* — 1926 — October 23
>   (Caesar Dies — BOOK)

THE RED FLAME OF ERINPURA
>   *Adventure* — 1927 — January 1
>   (The Red Flame of Erinpura — BOOK)

WHEN TRAILS WERE NEW
>   *Argosy-All-Story* — 1928 — October 27 to December 1
>   (Serial 6 parts)
>   (The Gunga Sahib — BOOK)
>   (When Trails Were New — BOOK)

THE WHEEL OF DESTINY
>   *Adventure* — 1928 — November 1

(The Gunga Sahib — BOOK)

THE BIG LEAGUE MIRACLE
Adventure — 1928 — November 15

ON THE ROAD TO ALLAH'S HEAVEN
Adventure — 1928 — December 1

GOLDEN RIVER
Adventure — 1929 — January 1

A TUCKET OF DRUMS
Adventure — 1929 — February 1

HO FOR LONDON TOWN
Argosy-All-Story — 1929 — February 2 to February 23
(Serial 4 parts)
(W.H. — BOOK)
(The Queen's Warrant — POCKETBOOK)

IN OLD NARADA FORT
Adventure — 1929 — February 15

ASOKA'S ALIBI
Argosy-All-Story — March 9 to March 23 — 1929 (Serial 3 parts)

BY ALLAH WHO MADE TIGERS
Argosy-All-Story — 1929 — April 27 to May 11 (Serial 3 parts)

FLAME OF CRUELTY
Romance — 1929 — August

THE INVISIBLE GUNS OF KABUL
Adventure — 1929 — October 1 to December 1 (Serial 5 parts)

(Cock O' the North — BOOK)

CONSISTENT ANYHOW
Adventure — 1930 — February 1

THE AFFAIR AT KALIGAON
Argosy — 1930 — May 24 to June 7 (Serial 3 parts)

KING OF THE WORLD
Adventure — 1930 — November 15 to February 15, 1931
(Serial 7 parts)
(Jimgrim — BOOK)

ELEPHANT SAHIB
Argosy — 1930 — December 6 to January 10, 1931
(Serial 6 parts)

BLACK FLAG
Adventure — 1931 — May 1

THE MAN ON THE MAT
Adventure — 1931 — August 1

THE BABU
Adventure — 1931 — October 1

THE EYE TEETH OF O'HARA
Adventure — 1931 — November 1
(The Valiant View — BOOK)

CASE 13
Adventure — 1932 — January 1

CHULL7UNDER GHOSE, THE GUILELESS
Adventure — 1932 — March 1

WATU (a reminiscence)
Adventure — 1932 — April 1

WHITE TIGERS
Adventure — 1932 — August 1 to August 15 (Serial 2 parts)

C.I.D.
Adventure — 1933 — March 1 to April 15 (Serial 4 parts)
(C.I.D. — BOOK)

THE MAN FROM POONCH
Argosy — 1933 — June 17
(The Valiant View — BOOK)

THE RED SEA CARGO
Adventure — 1933 — August

MILK OF THE MOON
Argosy — 1933 — September 17

CAMERA
Argosy — 1934 — January 6

THE GODS SEEM CONTENTED
Argosy — 1934 — September 15

BENGAL REBELLION
Blue Book — 1935 — January

BATTLE STATIONS
Adventure — 1935 — May 1
(Purple Pirate — BOOK)

CLEOPATRA'S PROMISE
Adventure — 1935 — June 15
(Purple Pirate — BOOK)

PURPLE PIRATE
>*Adventure* — 1935 — August 15
>(Purple Pirate — BOOK)

FLEETS OF FIRE
>*Adventure* — 1935 — October 1
>(Purple Pirate — BOOK)

THE WOLF OF THE PASS
>All Aces — 1936 — Hay

THE ELEPHANT WAITS
>Short Stories — 1937 — February 25

COMPANION IN ARMS
>*Adventure* — 1937 — November

ROMAN HOLIDAY
>Golden Fleece — 1938 — October

THE NIGHT THE CLOCKS STOPPED
>*Adventure* — 1941 — March

ODDS ON THE PROPHET
>Short Stories — 1941 — August 10

FULL MOON
>Famous Fantastic Mysteries — 1953 — February
>(Full Moon — BOOK)
>(There Was A Door — BOOK)

THE WALTER GALT
STORIES

Written under the pen-name of WALTER GALT, these tales are of Billy Blain, pugilist — all from *Adventure* Magazine

THE GONER
    1912 — February

THE SECOND RUNG 1912 — June

DORG'S LUCK 1912 — August

ACROSS THE COLOR LINE 1912 — October

LOVE AND WAR 1912 — November

THE TOP OF THE LADDER 1912 — December

ONE YEAR LATER 1913 — February

NOTHING DOING 1914 — September

THE RETURN OF BILLY BLAIN 1914 — November

BILLY BLAIN EATS BISCUITS
1916 — January

BILLY BLAIN'S ONIONS AND GARLIC
    1916 — February

Two articles under this pen-name

FRANCIS BANNERMAN – A MAN OF MYSTERY &
HISTORY 1912 – May

ELEPHANT HUNTING FOR A LIVING 1912 – July

MUNDY'S SAGAS

His sagas; with a story sequence of various characters by Dr. J. Lloyd Eaton

Talbot Mundy was a prolific writer of historical tales and stories of adventure-intrigue, his particular forte being tales of India and the Near East. Twelve of his novels are listed in *The Checklist of Fantastic Literature*, with themes of mysticism, black versus white magic, lost-race, and even true science fiction. Many others of his stories are borderline fantastics.

In the field of fantastic literature his works are highly prized (often highly priced, also) and many such readers find, possibly to their surprise, that they also enjoy his other stories. This may be due in some part to the fact that Mundy used the same characters over and over again, in novels in which each played the lead and as sub-characters in other novels. One keeps meeting old friends.

This leads to one difficulty in reading Mundy, however. If one is going to meet these characters, it is much more enjoyable to watch them develop from birth, so to speak — and not vice versa, like coming into a theatre in the middle of the picture. But, a reading sequence is a real difficulty. Each story is complete in itself, but the characters are re-shuffled into various combinations and any one of them may, and does, strike off into a novel of his own, only to reappear at a later date in some combination with other such characters. It is confusing, to say the least. To add to the confusion, all or nearly all of Mundy's stories first appeared in magazines, largely in *Adventure*, but later in *Argosy*.

As his popularity grew, his older stories were republished in book form, as well as each of his new novels, so that the date of publication of his books means nothing as far as reading chronology is concerned.

Before going any further, it may be interesting to digress a bit, and consider some of his earlier stories in *Adventure* Magazine, and more particularly as they apply to his books. No attempt is being made to give a complete listing of his magazine stories here. *Adventure* Magazine began publication in November 1910, but the earliest issue that I have for reference is that of August 1911. This contains a short story by Mundy, "The Phantom Battery." By this time he was publishing five to eight short stories per year. These early stories were mostly about the British Army and the most important was his "The Soul of A Regiment," (February 1913) a tale of native troops in the ill-fated first expedition against the Dervishes in Egypt, with a surprise, terrific, ending. This story was published as a book, "The Soul of A Regiment," (Alex Dulfer, San Francisco, 1925) and was anthologized by Arthur Sullivant Hoffman in *Adventure*'s *Best Stories — 1926* (Doran, New York, 1926). It was reprinted in Adventure Magazine in April 1917 and followed next month be a sequel, "The Damned Old Nigger." Three of his early novelettes (1913), "Hookum Hai," "For the Salt He Had Eaten," and "Machassan Ah," will be found in the book "Told in the East," (Bobbs-Merrill, Indianapolis, 1920). The first two concern the Sepoy Revolt and the third is a humorous story of the British Navy. All are good tales. The characters in the latter appear also in "An Arabian Night" (*Adventure*, November 1913). The first of his Indian hillman type stories is probably the short novel "The Letter of His Orders" (*Adventure*, September 1913). His first serial, "For the Peace of India" (*Adventure*, February to April 1914) was published in the book "Rung Ho" (Scribners, New York, 1914) and is another good story of the Sepoy Rebellion. In January and July 1914, appeared two stories about the Princess Yasmini, a character that he used extensively in later novels — as the lead, with King, with Ranjoor Singh, and in theJimgrim-Ramsden saga. The first of his sagas (Dick Anthony of Arran) was never published in book form. This series included eight novelettes and short novels, enough to fill four or five books, and appeared in successive issues of *Adventure* Magazine, beginning August 1914. These were very good adventure tales of a Scotch gentleman fighting for Iran against Old Russia, but are rather dated now. Following this, most of his novels appeared first in a magazine and were then immediately published in book form.

This brings us to the "Jimgrim-Ramsden Saga," the greatest of them all. If the early (and later) development of the associated characters is added, it continues through twenty-one books (twenty-two novels), and fifteen books (sixteen novels) for the actual Jimgrim-Ramsden stories.

This is not counting some eighteen novelettes and novels found in magazines only.

This Saga, in the main, is the story of James Schuyler Grim, (Jimgrim) a remarkable characterization, beginning as an American "Lawrence in Arabia" and evolving into a human but unapproachable high priest of the occult. There is Jeff Ramsden, the strong man and his closest friend, who with the Australian, Jeremy Ross, make up the triumvirate of Grim, Ross, and Ramsden, with their henchman Narayan Singh, the indomitable Sikh. (Who cuts throats with an outward thrust.) Later the multimillionaire, Meldrum Strange, hires them to fight evil. Then, Athelbert King, a hero of novels in his own right, joins up, making a quartet. Other characters from Mundy's novels appear — the seductive and dangerous Princess Yasmini; Cotswold Ommony, the forester of India; the Babu, Chullunder Ghose; the Gunga Sahib, and O'Hara.

READING SEQUENCE
FOR SAGAS

For an interesting reading sequence, the following is suggested.

> *** means excellent escapist reading — and fantastic
> (***) means excellent escapist reading — not fantastic
> Numbers indicate a book
> Indented numbers with letter mean magazine only
> Major characters, and their appearances, follow each title

(Ramsden tells many of the stories and is not listed except as necessary to connect the series.)

THE JIMGRIM-RAMSDEN, ET AL, SAGA

(***) 1. GUNS OF THE GODS (Bobbs-Merrill)
Yasmini 1

(***) 1a. A SOLDIER AND A GENTLEMAN
(*Adventure* January 1914)
Yasmini 2

(***) 1b. GULBAZ AND THE GAME (*Adventure* July 1914)
Yasmini 3

(***) 2. THE WINDS OF THE WORLD (Cassell)
Yasmini 4
Ranjoor Singh 1

(***) 3. HIRA SINGH (Bobbs-Merrill)
Ranjoor
Singh 2

*** 4. KING — OF THE KHYBER RIFLES
(Bobbs-Merrill)
King 1
Yasmini 5

(***) 5. JIMGRIM AND ALLAH'S PEACE
(Appleton-Century)
Jimgrim 1

(***) 5a. THE "IBLIS" AT LUDD (*Adventure* 1/10/22)
Jimgrim 2

(***)   6. TEE SEVENTEEN THIEVES OF EL-KALIL (Hutchinson)
Jimgrim 3

(***)   7. THE LION OF PETRA (Appleton-Century)
Jimgrim 4

(***)   8. THE WOMAN AYISHA (see THE HUNDRED DAYS — Century)
Jimgrim 5

(***)   9. THE LOST TROOPER (Hutchinson)
Jimgrim 6

(***)   10. THE KING IN CHECK (Appleton-Century)
Jimgrim 7

***   10a. A SECRET SOCIETY (*Adventure* 8/10/22)
Strange 1
Jimgrim 8

***   10b. MOSES AND MRS AINTREE (*Adventure* 1/10/22)
Strange 2
Jimgrim 9

***   11. THE MYSTERY OF KHUFU'S TOMB (Appleton-Century)
Strange 3
Jimgrim 10

***   12. THE CAVES OF TERROR (Hutchinson)
Yasmini 6
Strange 4
Ramsden
King 2

(**) 13. JUNGLE JEST (Century)
Ommony 1
King 3

(**) 14. THE MARRIAGE OF MELDRUM STRANGE
(Hutchinson)
Ramsden Strange 5
Ommony 2
Chullunder Ghose 1

** 15. OM; THE SECRET OF AHBOR VALLEY
(Bobbs-Merrill)
Ommony 3

(***) 16. THE HUNDRED DAYS (Century)
Jimgrim 11
King 4

*** 17. THE NINE UNKNOWN (Bobbs-Merrill)
Chullunder Ghose 2
Jimgrim 12
King 5

*** 18. THE DEVIL'S GUARD (Bobbs-Merrill)
Chullunder Ghose 3
Jimgrim 13

*** 19. JIMGRIM (Century)
Chullunder Ghose 4
Jimgrim 14

(***) 20. THE GUNGA SAHIB (Appleton-Century)
Chullunder Ghose 5
Quern 1

(***)   20a. THE WHEEL OF DESTINY (*Adventure* 11/1/28)

(This is roughly the same as the first four chapters of "The Gunga Sahib" From there on, any relationship between the book and the magazine stories seems to be coincidental.)

(***)   20b. THE BIG LEAGUE MIRACLE (*Adventure* 11/15/28)
        Quorn 2

(**)   20c. ON TEE ROAD TO ALLAH'S HEAVEN (*Adventure* 12/1/28)
        Quorn 3

(**)   20d. GOLDEN RIVER (*Adventure* 1/1/29)
        Quorn 4

(**)   20e. A TUCKET OF DRUMS (*Adventure* 2/1/29)
        Quorn 5

(***)   20f. IN OLD NARADA FORT (*Adventure* 2/15/29)
        Quorn 6

(***)   20g. ASOKA'S ALIBI (*Argosy*, 3 parts 3/9/29)
        Quorn 7

(***)   20h. THE AFFAIR AT KALIGAON (*Argosy*, 3 parts 5/24/30)
        Quorn 8

(***)   21. C.I.D. (Century)
        Chullunder Ghose 6

(**)   21a. THE BABU (*Adventure* 10/1/31)
        Chullunder Ghose 7
        O'Hara 1

(**)   21b. THE EYE TEETH OF O'HARA (*Adventure* 11/15/31)
               O'Hara 2

(***)   21c. CASE 13 (*Adventure* I/1/32)
               O'Hara 3
               Chullunder Ghose 8

(***)   21d. CHULLUNDER, THE GUILELESS (*Adventure* 3/1/32)
               Chullunder Ghose 9

(**)   22. THE RED FLAME OF ERINPURA (Hutchinson)
               Chullunder Ghose 10

MONTE, ET AL, SAGA

(**)   a. CAKES RESPECTS AN ADVERSARY (*Adventure* 12/3/18)

(***)   b. AMERICA HORN IN (*Adventure* 1/3/19)

(***)   c. JACKSON TACTICS (*Adventure* 2/18/19)

(***)   d. HEINE HORNS INTO THE GAME (*Adventure* 3/18/19)

(***)   e. THE END OF THE BAD SHIP BUNDESRATH (*Adventure* 4/18/19)

(***)   1. THE IVORY TRAIL (Bobbs-Merrill)

**   1a. THE SHRIEK OF DUM (*Adventure* 9/3/19)

***   1b. BARABBAS ISLAND (*Adventure* 10/18/19)

(**)   1c. IN ALEPPO BAZAAR (*Adventure* 1/19/20)

(***)   2. THE EYE OF ZEITOON (Bobbs-Merrill)

TROS SAGA

***   1. TROS OF SAMOTHRACE (Appleton-Century)

***   2. QUEEN CLEOPATRA (Bobbs-Merrill)

(***)   3. PURPLE PIRATE (Appleton-Century)

A FINAL NOTE FROM THE EDITOR

Three other books by Mundy are classed as fantasy, and, though not connected with the above sagas, are worthy of mention as fantastic.

***   1. BLACK LIGHT (Bobbs-Merrill)

***   2. FULL MOON (Appleton-Century)

***   3. THE THUNDER DRAGON GATE (Appleton-Century)

Good luck and best wishes to anyone so influenced by this listing as to attempt collecting these stories. A full purse will help.

FINIS

www.ingramcontent.com/pod-product-compliance
Lightning Source LLC
Chambersburg PA
CBHW031614040426
42452CB00006B/523

The Garden of Kama by Laurence Hope

The pseudonym for Adela Florence Cory Nicolson

Later published in the United States as India's Love Lyrics

Adela Florence Cory was born on 9th April 1865 at Stoke Bishop, Gloucestershire, the second of three daughters to Colonel Arthur Cory and Fanny Elizabeth Griffin. Adele was initially raised by relatives as her father was employed in Lahore in the service of the British army.

Eventually at 16, in 1881, she went to India to be reunited with her family. Her father was now the editor of the Lahore arm of The Civil and Military Gazette. Adela's sisters Annie Sophie and Isabel also has literary careers. Annie would go on to write popular, racy novels while Isabel assisted and then succeeded their father as editor of the Sind Gazette.

In April 1889 Adela married Colonel Malcolm Hassels Nicolson, a man twice her age and the commandant of the 3rd Battalion, the Baluch Regiment. Nicolson was a reputed action man and linguist and introduced his young wife to the glories of India, its customs, culture and food.

This deep immersion helped give the couple an eccentric reputation. In an expedition to the Zhob Valley in 1890 she disguised herself as a Pathan boy to follow her husband through the passes along the Afghan border. They would eventually live in Mhow for nearly a decade.

In 1901, she published 'Garden of Kama', which, a year later, was published in America with the title 'India's Love Lyrics'.

She originally attempted to pass the work off as translations of various poets, but this claim soon fell away. Still she shied away from any public recognition and used the publishing pseudonym of Laurence Hope to further shield herself.

Adela's poems were often suffused with imagery and symbols from the poets of the North-West Frontier and the Sufi poets of Persia and helped make her one of the most popular romantic poets of the Edwardian era with their themes of unrequited love, loss and often, the death that followed such an unhappy state of affairs.

Two months after Nicolson died in a prostate operation, Adela, who had been prone to depression since childhood, committed suicide by poisoning herself with perchloride of mercury.

Adela Florence Cory Nicolson died at the age of 39 on 4th October 1904 in Madras.

Index of Contents

"Less than the Dust"
"To the Unattainable"
"In the Early, Pearly Morning"
Reverie of Mahomed Akram at the Tamarind Tank

Verses
Song of Khan Zada
The Teak Forest
Valgovind's Boat Song
Kashmiri Song by Juma
Zira: In Captivity
Marriage Thoughts: By Morsellin Khan
To the Unattainable: Lament of Mahomed Akram
Mahomed Akram's Appeal to the Stars
Reminiscence of Mahomed Akram
Story by Lalla-ji, the Priest
Request
Story of Udaipore: Told by Lalla-ji, the Priest
Valgovind's Song in the Spring
Youth
When Love is Over. Song of Khan Zada
"Golden Eyes"
Kotri, by the River
Farewell
Afridi Love
Yasmini
Ojira, To Her Lover
Thoughts: Mahomed Akram
Prayer
The Aloe
Memory
The First Lover
Khan Zada's Song on the Hillside
Deserted Gipsy's Song: Hillside Camp
The Plains
"Lost Delight" After the Hazara War
Unforgotten
Song of Faiz Ulla
Story of Lilavanti
The Garden by the Bridge
Fate Knows no Tears
Verses: Faiz Ulla
Two Songs by Sitara, of Kashmir
Second Song: The Girl from Baltistan
Palm Trees by the Sea
Song by Gulbaz
Kashmiri Song
Reverie of Ormuz the Persian
Sunstroke
Adoration
Three Songs of Zahir-u-Din
Second Song
Third Song, Written During Fever